Poetry gives us the power to understa
and to write our future selves into bei

CW00409319

Secondhand Souls

Carlos Velez

Published by Scurvy Rickets, 2023.

SECONDHAND SOULS

First edition. July 8, 2023.

Copyright © 2023 Carlos Velez.

ISBN: 979-8223922506

Written by Carlos Velez.

.

Table of Contents

Dedication:

~

Elaine: For loving me and my words. For the life we create.

Nora: For making art that moves me.

Justus & Sam: For the many lessons on manhood.

Mom & Dad: For shaping the man I am in ways I realized, and ways I still haven't.

Alba: For reading what I wrote in high school with care and attention.

Jaedon: For writing in ways that remind me of me at that age, but better.

Steph: There are no words, though It hasn't stopped me from trying.

When It's Just Words

There aren't always words
But if you put them down
Anyway
If you just take the words
and let them anyway,
mistakes and all
Sometimes it says the truth
Sometimes it sets you free
And when it doesn't
When it's just words
Even then
It's space that was made
It's a moment spared
For yourself

Secondhand Souls

Inanimate objects can be such grief
When they carry such weight

I read a book about soul vessels in a secondhand shop
The items imbued with the souls of dearly departeds
They glowed red with energy
They must have been heavy too
With the weight of memory
History

I unpacked mundane things from a box
We packed up, in our old home
Glass jars
Plastic pitchers
A damaged cheese grater that had limped through the last of its usefulness
None were special
You wouldn't put a soul
A beautiful soul
In a metal soup bowl, with a damaged plastic lid

But we put so much soup in that bowl
Maybe if you put enough love in it
a metal soup bowl can be a soul vessel
Certainly the soup was full of love
We made it together
So many soups

It's hard to picture her in my mind
But a soup bowl is easy
And with it, she appears
Ladling leftovers for tomorrow

She's laughing of course
She's a laugh-whore just like me
We laugh
We laugh all the time
We made soup while we laughed

The soup bowl was heavy
I can't believe it didn't glow red
It's hard to pass it on
To put it away in a box
To let it go
It remembers her
But it's no use with no lid
It's not expensive or hand-made or beautiful
It was functional and it has done its work
You can't keep everything
There must be a letting go

But I won't let go of the picture it gave me
Her laughing
I'll write it into my memory
In ink and on paper
Into the cloud
Into millions of pixels and millions of bytes
Maybe a soup bowl can be inanimate
but also give me a loving laugh
Anytime I want it
Maybe it can fill in a piece of an old puzzle
That has so many missing pieces

Grief, piece by piece
Peace, grief by grief

This House

This house is quiet with sleep
and the ti-tick of clocks in syncopation
This house is dark
and my little light casts looming shadow to write by
This full house squeezes tight in the waking day
With five bodies
and five voices
and five hearts
all expanding
This house becomes soup with feelings
Simmering boiling overflowing
Cooling calming filling soothing
This house is musical with piano plinks
and unrestrained cackles
This house is wild with wandering plants
and sunflower walls
This house is sweet with love
and warm with affection
This house is safe
Inside this house is home

A Blacksmith's Hands

Striking while the iron is hot
Is not a simple task
It begins with danger

Fire, ever-hungry and hostile
Tamed with a delicate touch
Crafted tools, used with care
Purpose and poise to pull potential from the forge
To rest it upon hard, solid steel
Unyielding, unbreaking

It is a clearness of vision for what is
And what can be
In glowing, molten metal

Geometry of angles
Physics of force
Position, momentum, intention
And in fleeting moments
A sure, straight strike
A recoil, recycled into re-momentum
Another strike, holding the heat in for one more fleeting moment
Before glowing molten metal dulls
And cools once more
Returned to the forge

Forty thousand hammer strikes a day a blacksmith make
Poised and ready to strike
While the iron is hot

I'm A Man

I'm a man, he said
His eyes were glass hard and offended
Don't expect—

His voice was barbed sharp and defensive
The mere thought
of balance with his feminine
Struck cold fear and sparked a hot reaction

Pretending to be a whole man
Clutching at wounds

Standing Room

On the shortest day of the longest year
Somehow we made it here
Looking around I see that we
have reached the edge of our fears
Some of us scream into futures and voids
Some of us leap into air
Some of us can't find a solid ground
and some of us can only despair

Because change starts in our feet
and our toes are long-broken
and our heels are loud with rust
and some of us see that everything's changed
Because ultimately we're not afraid of change
Because clowns became scary and our witches are wise
and doing what you love makes time fly

On the shortest day of the longest year
Those who understand have no room for fear
No time for bullshit
No time to fix it for those who abuse it
No place for dead weight
No respect for dead traits
No patience for dead fates
The hour is dead late

On the shortest day of the longest year
We're here
We know where we stand
Or we stand in our fears

11

The Infinite Moment

The human mind had long ago been digitized
Daily life reproduced through fractals of code
And clusters of processors
At first it kept the pace of natural life
The two worlds in time's sync
But the processors got faster
The connections more efficient
The code more innovative
And the human mind ever kept the pace
Plugged in
Supplemented
Augmented
Perfected

By the time we knew about the meteor
We were already trading hours for days
Life was fast
Faster than ever
Processing life in fast forward
The world around us slowed
A week in a day
A month in the next
And always
Doom fell slow from the sky

Our addiction became our only option
Our rescue
We couldn't help it
Suddenly we had a deadline
All of us
And we saw it coming
We added more processors

We invented new technologies
Life sped
Faster than ever
A season of sun
Years of summer
Brilliant new architectures of code rose in moments
And crumbled into decay moments later
Always replaced by something stronger
Faster
Ever faster

We turned our backs on the sky
We closed our eyes to the world
And opened ourselves to the universe we created
Letting it in
And burying ourselves in its womb

Time became a divide in history
Life when time rushed
Foam and rapids over rocks and stubborn weeds
Life when time stopped
One long, infinite horizon

Time became a legend
The ever-approaching meteor did too
The infinite moment grew and grew
Expanding our universe into forever
Life became eternal
A moment before its doom

Invisible Ink

I've never imagined a tattoo that I had to have
I'm not sure why
Always kinda wanted a sleeve though
A sleeve says something
Or it's a chance to
A tattoo can be anything
But a sleeve has got to be You

When I met Elaine
She didn't have a sleeve
(still doesn't, but she's getting closer)
A bird sang on one shoulder
And babes swam in mother's arms on the other
Mother and nature
Soon a woman with her moon, un-shamed and in her strength
Stretched down her arm
Beautiful fire red and thin black lines
Her tattoos are not a sleeve,
But very clearly her

Tattoos have never been clear like that to me
What lasts as long as a tattoo?
Religion did not
Marriage did not
Does a tattoo have to last?

What if it was just funny?
Like...
A button on the back of my hand
A really pressable-looking button
A big red one obviously

With cross-hatched shadows
and a tempting shiny white glimmer
Like it was reflecting a spotlight
Begging you
Press. The. Button.
And when you do...
Something unexpected happens
...my tongue sticks out
or...I hop and clap my feet
or...my eyes go crossed
or...maybe I just say something nice

Maybe the tattoo could be something nice
Like...
"You're lovely because"
In elegant, simple print
And when people ask me "...because why?"
I'll tell them because why
Because I had fun with you
Because you considered me
Because I feel safe talking to you
Because you have the best laugh
Because you know how to let me be sad

Of course, a tattoo can be sad
It can be a tribute
A memory
I wouldn't want a tattoo like that to be formal
No faces or names
I'm not a tombstone
If I wrote grief and loss and love into a tattoo
It would be music
Maybe as notes and staff
Maybe transformed into new colors and shapes

I've seen music as blocks and lights
spirals, patterns, and outlines
Always carrying the weight of the hammers and strings

But maybe a tattoo doesn't have to be so heavy
It could just be a single moment
Or a whole week!
A box on my arm for every day that ends in "Y"
Coffee on Thursday? Let me check my shhhhedule
I can pencil you in...
- err, scratch that. I'm going to need a pen.
Don't go canceling on me

I don't know really
There are a million great tattoos
How do you pick one?
What if it picks you?

If a tattoo picked me
It would surely be one of a kind
And a little vulnerable
Bold and beautiful
Maybe it would cover my arm
And I'd get that full sleeve after all
Maybe it would say something important
You might look at it and know just who I am
About something particular
Love or art or grief
Connection or kindness

Whatever it might be
I still can't see it
Maybe it's drawn with invisible ink

I Knew A Man

I knew a man
who cared more for his rightness
than the facts
An intelligent man
whose intelligence failed to perceive the truth
through the fog of fear

Fear deformed every input
- Bad data makes bad calculations
Fear compromised his output
- Bad resources make bad results
Fear distorted his Self
- Bad components make system failure

I knew a man
ruled by his fear
He hurt people
He hurt people he loved, in fact
His fear turned his intentions to betrayals
Turned blessings to curses
The harms of his fear spread wide
and sank deep

I left him
Now his fears are gone from my life
I cannot erase what already is
But the harm done gets older
and weaker
every day

Witchcraft and Wizardry

There is a magic
in the layering of the senses

A sniff
A glance
A laugh
A caress
A savor

Life is many, many moments
The way we consume each one
Matters
The way we produce them
matters too
What looks beautiful
may feel harsh
What sounds sweet
may taste bitter

A proper magic is mindful
of all our senses
In the sum of the whole
is a whole other creation
A kind of life, all of its own

It terrifies us
To be wholly, completely cast into our moments
We're terrified that we can create something as powerful as life
That we can do magic after all
Terrified that our spells might be broken

But our spells are broken
Our lives are divided
Our senses are isolated
and magic does not exist
So everyone says

Except for witches

Fresh Cut Flowers Sold Here

Down in Pixie Hollow
Just a little old place
There's flowers to smell
and mushrooms
Books to love
and cute critters too
Birdsong and bird friends
and robin's eggs so blue

What stories these trees could tell-
——And stories go best with tea!
What bridges to cross
Briars and thickets
Naps in the shade with the
summertime crickets

What dreams this hollow must make-
——And tea goes best with cake!
Imagine the stories
Just picture the dreams
Where all is fantastic and
Just how it seems

Imagine the world such a place must create
Down in Pixie Hollow
Just a little ol' place

——Are you gonna finish that cake?

Done Did

There may only be a minute.
So what is there to do?
What can be done?
Must it be done?
Is it the doing?
Or the did?
Is it done?
Is it?
Yes.
It is.

1500 Seconds

Time is marching past on these New York City streets
idling along, looking in the windows
720 seconds, the mannequins in the fur coats
stand in stiff poses as I think about bowling
This, my ambition, and father would hit the roof
Four hundred seconds, don't walk flash to walk
3 minutes left till ka-tet and I fade
and I fade and I fade as 'Dr. Love' plays
on the boombox, the Chicano stops and I fade
That black man in a panama hat, he yells 'oh my god, he's kilt!'
She'll drop the bag and the bag will be spilt
I'll see this from where I'll be lying in the street
with blood soaking pants. What's happening to me?
But I can't stop walking because this is a nightmare
53 seconds and the priest will be there
The hands that pushed me forward into street and into death
'Step aside, let me through' as I take my last breath
40 seconds left walk, don't walk, on and off
Big blue Cadillac on 5th & 43rd
'I'm going to die' but I can't stop it now
and inside her bag is the doll that will fall
6 seconds now. 76 Sedan de Ville
means to scat the intersection with a snarl from its grille
3 seconds left, the man in black was lunging forward
As 'Dr. Love' begins, never getting to the chorus
2 seconds and the Cadillac comes into the lane
1 second breath stopped short and I wait
0

Making Messes

It feels like I should wait
Until I have something to say
Something deep, you know?
Or beautiful
Maybe something wrenching with honesty

But really
I keep finding that waiting for inspiration
Feels a lot like procrastination
That I do more and better work
When I do something
Anything
Even if it's a mess

It's easier to clean up a mess
Or do it all over again
Than it is to do it right
And that the more I jump in and work
Making messes, crashing, failing
Even scrapping what I've done
I flex new muscles
My tools get sharper
My process gets clearer
And I keep making new things
Better

With Live Ammunition

It's her third time with live ammunition
It feels old
She feels old as glass shatters
The mosaic spreads across the ground
a glistening puddle of bullshit and tears
and grief and bullshit fears
She sighs and swears lightly
She cries and squeezes tightly
She flies straight and smashes
and more glass crashes in a spray
and a splatter
a tinkling clatter
Another squeeze, another pop
Another sigh
Finally it stops

Bite Down Hard

Bite down
Hard

Even if your tongue bleeds
Even if it swells and fills your throat
Even if you feel like you can't breathe

Swallow
You can't afford the risk
Freedom is an idea
Not a reality
Not a given
Not for you
You weren't born that way

Bite down
Hard
Stay safe

But be careful
It needs a way out
You can't hold on to it
You have to choose
...carefully...
where you can be free

What Sticks

We live on
in unexpected ways
we'll never be able to predict
for those who can't imagine a life
without us

It is not our greatest feats
or most impressive successes
that linger
It's the small, personal touches
that strike deep
It's the words we don't bother to consider
The moments that didn't warrant a photo
at the time
Little actions that will
Someday
Trigger a shockwave in their hearts
we never intended

These things that define us
Every day
The auto-pilot reactions
The habitual behaviors
These are what stick
These are what we must shape with intention
These will be our legacy
for those who love us most

Washburn Connection

I've been here before
But this space
Is not mine
Not like it is his
He connected where
I could not
It was a moment in lifetimes
For him it has been
Lifetimes
But here
In this space
At least in this moment
His connection
Is mine

When I Was A Boy

When I was a boy
I sought the single truth

As a young man
I knew the single truth in my heart

I became a grown man
and realized many truths
Outside myself

In moments of wisdom
I grasp equal and opposite truths
and hold them
Calmly
In hand

Old Man Goat

He's wrinkled and gnarly
Old, strong, and bent
Quiet, but a storm cloud
Old man goat
I want to be just like him

Tape Collection

Music feels like the frame on which I've hung nearly every recollection, giving me access to large files of childhood memories. Each song, each note, has a memory attached to it.
- Ben Folds (A Dream About Lightning Bugs - A Life of Music and Cheap Lessons)

My memory is vague, and non-visual
Music is a device that can sharpen memories and uncover the forgotten
Songs remind me of who I was
and what life looked like during the days
when I first heard it or had it
On regular rotation
The tapes and cds and downloads and apps and playlists expose me
They remember me

Music is self Mutilation
Music is self Masturbation
Music is self Examination
Music is self Medication
Music is self Salvation
Music is self Education
Music is self Inspiration
Music is self Creation

STORIES, MEDITATIONS, AND REFLECTIONS

~

The afternoon sun was golden. It speckled his face and she smiled. She loves me, he thought. He knew it. It was tangible. Heavy, like a warm blanket on a freezing morning. Her eyes said what she hadn't admitted yet. Love.

He hadn't admitted it either. It was- complicated. For the one, he was still homeless. For the two- he was lost. Love was familiar, but not what he had expected.

His eyes closed and he went deep as he thought of it. His hands were on her legs, and she had smiled that smile. He felt the little vibrations in his fingertips, on her skin. He watched the little expenditure of energy glow, in his mind, and run through her limbs. Love's blood, circulating. It shined in her eyes. She loves me, he thought, and I love her. He didn't say it, but she felt it kindle in his hands and spread through her. She shivered.

"What shall we do tonight, darling?" she asked. She wanted what she wanted. To be seen in love. To be beautiful. To make beautiful love.

"Music," he said. "Let's see a show. You can wear a dress." She loved music. He loved watching her love music. She listened with her body and her soul.

"I can wear my witchy dress!" she said, excited now.

He smiled. "Your witchy dress? Yes please. Which would that be?"

"The violet dress." Her eyes smoldered. His eyes smoldered.

He really did love her. It radiated around them, between them. Why now? He had only just arrived in town. He had yet to make a life here. He had plans, and dreams. He wasn't supposed to be in love.

She would be in that violet dress though. And he did love her in violet. He wasn't afraid of love. He never had been. That was the beautiful half of the coin, and he knew its shine. He flipped it again and it came up love.

"I love you in that dress," he smiled and winked. He was up and heading to the tea cart to refill their cups.

She was barely out of step with his casual use of the word. "You love me out of this dress."

He could see her grin in his mind. He could see her in his mind. She was beautiful. And she was right. He did love her out of that dress. He loved her in every place, and every time. When they talked, when they ate. He loved her in the sun, and in the darkest corners. He loved her in bed, and in music and mornings, naps and adventures.

He poured her tea. Cream and honey. Whiskey. He poured his tea the same. He sipped and felt the tea seep into dry, weary places. Perfect. He carried the cups back. She was still smiling exactly as he knew she had been. He looked at her. He said it, but no words came out. I love you. She felt it.

He didn't know what will, but he knew what was. Love.

Nina

In her autobiography, Nina Simone talked at length about her connection with the audience when she performs. A tangible energy. She would send it with her voice and her piano through the room and people become ecstatic. As a child, she played gospel music in her mother's church. Her mother was the Minister and she gave powerful messages that stirred the congregation up on their feet. She led revivals full of ecstatic people, praising and worshiping with furious energy. Nina played for them. She fed off their energy and fed it back to them. She was viscerally aware, even then, of her energetic connection with the audience.

She commanded absolute attention when she performed. If an audience did not give it, she would walk out. She was known for it. She knew what she was, and "jazz singer" didn't begin to cover it. She was a revivalist. When she performed, she was connecting purely and powerfully to her own soul. A meditative state. A flow state. She was in hyper-focus, doing what she had long-since mastered. She was in a pure soul-connected state and she emptied herself for the audience. She commanded a rapturous audience. Take the journey into her soul and out into the worlds she creates or don't. She's not cocktail hour music. She's the only thing that matters right now.

"I'm not a blues singer, I'm a diva."

"I want to shake people up so bad that when they leave a nightclub where I've performed, I just want them to be to pieces."

"I'll tell you what freedom is to me: no fear. I mean, really, no fear!"

"I think that the artists who don't get involved in preaching messages probably are happier—but you see, I have to live with Nina, and that is very difficult."

"As a political weapon, it has helped me for 30 years defend the rights of American blacks and third-world people all over the world, to defend them with protest songs. To move the audience to make them conscious of what has been done to my people around the world."

Music and Magic

My intention is to fill this home
With love and light
Music and magic
To stride forth
Honest and confident
To put down roots
And extend myself
Into connection with
Different peoples

Not Yet

I remember making sense of the drums in 7th grade, listening to Weezer's self-titled *"Blue Album"* in my room while I played hacky sack.

I decided it would be a good album to drum along with for practice. Since those are the songs where my brain first understood the drums, it would make sense for my body to do the same.

In particular it was the last song on the album, *Only In Dreams*. It has the simplest drum pattern you could ask for, but it keeps changing in the simplest and most predictable way...1 beat per measure increases to 2 beats per measure, then to 4, then 8, and finally 16. The kick and the snare? Boom - Kack - Boom - Kack (or Boots - Cats if you prefer).

It gets big and intense, and it gets small and quiet. But it just keeps doing so in these inevitable, completely predictable doubles and halves.

The ending is the most satisfying part though. After a straightforward intro/verse/chorus/verse/chorus it dies down to almost nothing but the bassline and a single, delicate hit of the ride cymbal. The drums are just a drip of water. Then it slowly builds...drip drip, drip drip drip drip...in that same predictable doubling pattern it has used through the whole song. It just keeps going, taking its time, drawing the build-up out over this ever-so-slowly-intensifying guitar solo, not shredding, not going wild with scales of notes, just persisting more, and more, and more. Eventually the drums are pounding, *pounding*, **pounding**. It's still simple, but it demands that steady persistence of the body that it just isn't used to.

I pounded along, *pounded* along, **pounded** along, waiting for the final moment of build-up when the snare drum finally, and so satisfyingly breaks the pattern...kack kack-kack kack-kack-kack CRASH!

But...I missed it. 😕

This is why I'm not a drummer yet. A drummer can't miss that moment. It's the climax of the song. It's the climax of the past 45 minutes of the entire album. My body doesn't know that simple, engine-persistence yet, even though my brain could play it all day.

Not yet.   .

Overtones In The Air

I get this feeling sometimes. I walk to the piano with this feeling like a haze coming over me. Or coming out of me. I often just "know" when a piece of music is going to flow. I feel it.

Sometimes I grab my phone to record it, hoping all the while that I don't break the trance...like trying to keep yourself from waking from a dream you want to stay in. Sometimes I don't grab my phone and I just let the song roll out into the air and evaporate before its audience...a one-time only story, never to be repeated. Sometimes I really wish I'd grabbed my phone and could "have" the song I just played, so I can produce it and release it, a finished product.

But it's important to let some of these songs blow in the wind. It's important to not document everything. To sometimes let music be nothing except my time with the piano, my fingers on the keys, the overtones in the air, the space each soundwave fills in the home, and the ears that are there to hear it. A unique moment for a unique audience, even when I'm the only soul around to hear it.

Happiness

Art is the expression and reflection of life
Science is the study and experimentation of life
Work is the application and improvement of life
Play is the joy and freedom of life
Happiness is the result of all the above
and recognizing there is little difference between them

Had To

I have a box full of recordings from when I was in my late teens and early twenties. Only a couple were helpfully labeled. The rest have been a mystery for most of two decades. I got a tiny boombox last year to hear what was on them. Now, during quarantine, I'm digitizing them.

There's a practice session from my old punk band, a handful of songs by friends of mine, and acoustic guitar stuff I was working on back then. It was so early in our time as musicians. Much of it is not very good, some of it is, a lot of it shows clues to the artists we would grow to be.

We had to suck to get better. We had to write painfully bad songs to write songs that sounded okay but were boring. We had to write boring songs to write interesting ones. We had to write interesting songs, to write good songs. We had to write songs to write great songs.

I am strong
I am creative
I am home
I am creative

I have the love I deserve
I deserve the love I have
I am creative

I am kind
Rest is welcome
I am creative

I am loved
I am creative
I work hard
I am creative

A Precautionary Tale

Tears sting my eyes, and my chest heaves with weight and freedom. Grief and peace. Loss and wonder. An old tale. Anew. A Precautionary.

I haven't known why I named this piece of music *Precautionary*, until perhaps now. The name, like the tale, knows fear and longing. What we all long for. A place. Family. Home.

It is hard to live with loss. It is stressful to live with lack. It is debilitating to live with the possibility of having everything you ever wanted...as long as the chaos is silent for once. As long as you don't lose it, or crush it.

Precautionary is a pandemic story. 2020. The Covids. A dozen or so minutes of music in April, recorded in a tiny living room, with twinkle lights, in a tiny little yellow house. It glowed like love in the midst of desolation. I sat at my keyboard and played this, then that, then this other thing. It fit together in a strange way, if I held it just right. These very different feelings, vibes, stories.

Turning a dozen or so minutes of playing piano into a symphonic story took hours and days, then weeks and months, here and there over two years. I played and studied new instruments, read books on orchestration and composition, trained on multiple software, bought plugins, wrestled with technical problems, and listened to it over and over and over. Analyzing and imagining.

It is orchestrated as a symphony, but it is not classical music. There are no rules that govern its form, its direction, or its voice. It is not particularly original or bizarre. Except maybe that bit in the middle. But every note pulls at me. It's my story. Pictures of the life unfolding to me in 2020. In the midst of devastation. In the midst of illness. The pieces of a mysterious puzzle just starting to finally come together and show what was possible. The fear that brought went deep...that such beautiful futures may not flourish in the chaos.

This music takes me through wonder and tentative exploration, into harsh clumsy failure, down to childish joy and earnest intention. It carries me on through rushing leaps and wild adventure. It cascades into chaos, and rides it down to an invigorated, ambitious peace, and tries again with a gentler, more tender touch. After all is done, and all are tucked away into sleep and rest, it drifts me through home and love, fulfilled, satisfied with how precautionary possibilities have bloomed into lush realities.

From the loves of your life

Healing, healing, from the loves of your life
Strength, strength, from the loves of your life
Peace, peace, from the loves of your life
Magic, magic, from the loves of your life

A Tumble of Love

Every morning he wakes and makes his way. More stooped, more gray. More wrinkled. He shuffles more than he steps. He makes his way.

He turns on the stove, missing the hiss and click of the old gas models. Water in the pot, beans in the grinder. Coffee is a process. He used to weigh the beans, meticulous. Now he knows it by feel. The same beans, same grinder, same two coffee drinkers.

He hears her longer, shuffling strides, murmuring to the plants and the rats and the crab as she does every morning. Her familiars. She sweeps into the kitchen as the kettle rattles to a boil. He lets the kettle grumble and spit, a smile wrapping his face in well-engraved lines and wrinkles. He kisses her, and he has that same old feeling. A canoe in a misty lake, the world beyond the gray riding on gentle lapping waves, further and further away. Each pulse of the kiss pulling them closer together, and further into the silver mist.

He slaps her gently on the butt and winks, then, finally, frees the angry kettle from its torment, glad he no longer has to remember to turn the burner off. Not that these new stoves could burn anything; and a good thing too or the house may long ago have been ashes where he stood. He eyes her as she fetches a nearly identical kettle, only more scorched and weary, and fills it with cold water, singing in the window, for all the world a song-bird in his heart.

She has always sung. She enchanted him many years ago. But he's glad she sings even more as they've gotten older. She "Ran out of shits back in 2020," as she was fond of saying, followed by "and I've never seen clearer!" if she was feeling particularly saucy.

He pours. The pour is the good part. All of it needs to be right of course. Good, fresh beans, coarse grind. Clean water, right temperature. All the best ingredients. But the pour is where the magic lives, the casting of the spell. She takes her kettle out into the living room. She likes using it to water plants for the same reason he likes it for coffee: the perfect pour. The stem curved in a swan's neck from the bottom of the kettle. A slender graceful arch of stainless steel and a thin, full stream of slow water, easily poured with only a slight twist of the wrist.

He listens to her move through the house as he watches the steaming water fall like grace on coffee grounds, thirsty, thankful dunes. He pours counter-clockwise, spiraling a pattern like impatients, blossoming out of the swirling grounds and water. He stops after the first 75 grams of water. Well, after the grounds have been saturated; it just always lands on 75.

The steam wafts slowly up and past his face. He breathes it in and his shoulders settle from tension he hadn't noticed as he watches the coffee ground dunes reach the peak of their bloom and then retract with a shudder of relief. The grounds now saturated, off-gassed, and ready, he pours in earnest. Slow and methodical, spiraling patterns. It slices through the tender bloom, destroying it and blooming anew with fresh vigor.

The coffee tinkles in the glass. Its hour-glass shape moves coffee grounds and water through its crucible, making new, and fresh. The plinks turn to little plops and mingle with her song for sweet moments before he hears the patio door slide. Song birds and wind join the music and her voice fades back into a low breath as she walks out onto the deck to water more plants and wait for him, and his process.

Six more times around and we'll be there, he thinks. He pours six more impatients into the roiling mixture and watches it begin to settle as the last grams of water drop straight down the center. Two small coffee mugs, a generous splash of whole cream. The plops of coffee slow behind him as he puts the cream away.

It's a perfectly timed dance for a tune he knows by heart. It glides over the glass spout in the final pour, coffee into cream, blending dark and light into inextricable balance. It hums in his body as he shuffles his way out of the kitchen. He moves slowly; his hands have never been exactly steady. But no coffee spills. He steps in time with the music. It laps in beat against the sides of the coffee mugs. It scrapes the wood floor with his slippers. It bumbles low in his throat. It calls from outside - the birds and the air. It sings to the plants and waits in a seat by a table.

He puts the coffee on the table and looks up at her as he turns to sit. Her eyes are on him. So often, her eyes are on him. He is beautiful and he knows. She has always told him.

The song wells up. It's so loud and wondrous in her eyes.

He sits close, bodies pressed together and warm. The song settles into waves around them.

Legacy

My legacy isn't in my genes. My legacy isn't a staking of territory to say *I was here, and part of me will always be here.* The world will move on without me, the world will forget me, and that is inevitable and right, no matter how many kids I could have.

My legacy is the impact I have on everyone around me. My legacy is the example I set as a role-model, for better and for worse. My legacy is my mood, and my words, and my actions on my bad days. My legacy is the safe places I create for others. My legacy is in the harshness and judgments I project. My legacy is my failures; the failures that hurt me and the people I love, and the failures that I face honestly and grow from. My legacy is in my ability to be vulnerable, and to hold boundaries. It's in my willingness to express and create myself. My legacy is rooted in the support I give others.

I realized that it's more important that I be a man, than that I be a father. The world doesn't need more people. It's overburdened already. But damn does the world need more men. These past few years, being a man in the lives of children I love and care for, have challenged me to be a role model in ways that I was unprepared for, and in ways that I had to grieve not having an example to look up to.

I've heard the phrase "It's easy to be a father, it's hard to be a dad." But really, it's hard to be a man. It isn't just dads that need to be role models and safe places to children. It's all of us. Like it or not, they see us. Like it or not, we are role models. Our genes have no impact on the world. We ARE our impact on the world. That is our legacy.

In some ways it is more terrifying to try to be a good man than just about anything else a man might do. It is easier to rage at the world, rage at our children, rage at every messed up thing that breeds hopelessness and nihilism. Too fucking bad. Be a man.

Being a man means failing. It means being honest about it. It means being hurt and vulnerable. It means growing from it and trying again. It means creating safety for ourselves and others. It means nurturing living things. It means impacting the world - not in a grand way, not at a societal level, not as some hero who sees the truth that no one else sees and fixes the world's problems. It means impacting the world one little person at a time, with every mood, word, and action, every day.

I've learned to be a man from women. Because being a good man means being a good human. I've learned to be a man from my peers and from kids because being a man has nothing to do with age or elder wisdom. I've learned to be a man from people who show courage every day in their own lives; the courage to be honest with themselves and change because being a good man requires the wisdom to question our own assumptions and biases. To accept and reconcile many truths, even as they appear, on the surface, to conflict with each other. Celebrating victories, and celebrating failure as both lead us towards the next stage in our growth, and the next iteration of our impact on our loved ones, on the people we know, and on all the people we didn't know were watching us. Being a man requires empathy and constant growth.

There's no such thing as stasis in the universe. Life strives, or it falls into entropy. Being a man means striving to be a better man, always.

Ingram Content Group UK Ltd.
Milton Keynes UK
UKHW040845100723
424852UK00001B/85